Sneaker & Me

A heartwarming story of an adopted black cat
By Barbara Bounds

Copyright © 2014 Barbara Bounds

About the Author

Since 1988, Barbara Bounds and her husband, Raymond, have been the owners and operators of Belspur Oaks Pet Crematory, Inc. Located on Florida's Gulf Coast, their company has been serving the animal community by offering dignified private cremations, grief support materials, and personalized memorial products.

For a number of years, she and her husband have also been involved in a community pet loss grief support group called Bentley's House. The purpose of this group is to give grieving pet owners an opportunity to share their memories of their pets with other animal lovers in a safe, nonjudgmental, and supportive atmosphere.

In helping thousands of grieving pet owners say their final goodbyes to their beloved pets, Barbara noticed that the same questions seem to always be asked: "Do you have pets of your own?" and "Have you ever experienced the passing of a beloved and cherished pet?"

So, it was with the recurrence of these questions and the informal sharing of these experiences with her pets that Sneaker and Me came to fruition.

Barbara's hope for this book is twofold. First, she would like the memory of the relationship that she shared with Sneaker to be both inspirational and therapeutic to those who are either considering adopting a shelter cat or experiencing or about to endure the loss of a beloved pet.

And second, it carries with it an underlying theme: responsible pet ownership is for the entire life of the pet.

Dedication

This book is dedicated to my beloved and cherished cat, Sneaker, who displayed the meaning of unconditional love, gentleness, and gratitude-the kind that could only come from an adopted, small, black cat.

Sneaker's incredible life began as a shelter cat at a local humane society.

It was there that I first met my cat Sneaker. I was there on a mission to find a cat and give it a forever home.

What I didn't expect was to adopt a small, black cat who would become the most beautiful animal I would ever own.

I can vividly remember entering the cat room of the shelter. It was nothing like the kind of cat shelters that exist today. There were no cat condos or catios for the cats to lounge in, but only a chain link fence keeping many cats corralled in a small area.

Because there were so many different kinds of cats, it was hard for me to choose which cat to consider adopting.

The staff member assisting me pointed Sneaker out to me. She took Sneaker out of the cage and allowed us some time to get acquainted.

After I held her for a while, I decided to put her back into the cage and chose another cat.

As I was playing with the other cat, I expressed that I really didn't want to adopt Sneaker because she was black and I was, perhaps, a bit superstitious.

It was at this point that the staff member began explaining to me that Sneaker was a good-natured cat and that she had fostered her for a while before returning her to the shelter. She also mentioned that Sneaker had given birth to several kittens, but they were born sickly and none had survived.

What she said made me feel sad for Sneaker, and, at that moment, I recall hearing Sneaker screaming and howling at me to take her back out of the cage. As I turned to look in the direction of the noise, I realized that she had climbed to the top of the cage in a desperate and final attempt to get my attention.

The staff member then turned to me and said, "That cat wants to go home with you!"

So, I took Sneaker back out of the cage for a second time, and, immediately after I kneeled down, she jumped into my lap to let me know that she, indeed, had chosen me to give her a forever home.

It was at that point that I knew in my heart that she was the cat for me. She had chosen me!

I decided to fill out the adoption application and, upon quick approval,

brought her home!

I soon realized that we were inseparable and that I really needed to give her a better name than the one that the shelter had given her, which was "Blackie."

One day, while I was outside hanging the laundry, it seemed that every step I took, that cat was under my feet. Because she was so insistent on following me everywhere, I would occasionally accidentally step on her little paws.

I felt terrible when this happened and gradually became frustrated because I couldn't understand why she would continue to cause me to trip over her and risk getting herself injured.

So after nearly tripping over her for what seemed like the 100th time, I decided to name her "Sneaker." I concluded that it would be the perfect name for a cat who was always "clinging to my sneakers."

Over the course of several years, my family grew in size. Two children joined our family, a boy and a girl. Sneaker loved the children and seemed very protective of them, especially when they were sick.

She loved to participate in whatever the kids were doing and "share" their toys when they were playing.

On several occasions, she could be found with her eyes wide open, chasing and pouncing on the Match Box cars speeding around my son's race track set.

In time, our family adopted a grey, tiger-striped cat we named Tinkerbell. We loved him, too. He was not quite as adventurous as Sneaker was, but could take credit, too, for joining her in at least one amazing encounter involving an opossum. Yes, an opossum!

An orphaned baby opossum had found its way into our garage. Sneaker and Tinkerbell took him in, kept him safe, and shared their kitty food with him. They even trained him to use the litter box!

I never had a clue that this was happening until

late one night, I heard muffled peculiar noises coming from the garage. It was then that I discovered that our cats had been sheltering an opossum.

Imagine my surprise to find two kitties and one baby opossum feeding from the same dish!

Sneaker was always curious about the outdoors, especially after dark when the night creatures came calling. Living next to a nature preserve provided many opportunities for these nighttime encounters and for Sneaker to test her curiosity.

Out of their daytime dens, these critters travelled along our yard, communicating in their various animal languages. At one point, this proved to be too enticing for Sneaker to resist. So one night, her curiosity lead her to the top of the pool cage!

Yes, that's right. Sneaker dove from the top of the pool cage, tearing through the pool screen, and belly flopping right into the swimming pool!

At the time, I was sound asleep in my bed. But upon hearing some commotion and a loud splash, I got up and looked outside my sliding glass door.

There I saw an animal that resembled a wet rat. I started shrieking to my husband, "It's a rat, it's a raccoon, it's I don't know what! It's scary!" As my husband looked more closely, he said, "Barb, it's Sneaker!"

Poor thing! We brought her inside, towel dried her, and hoped that she would never explore the top of the pool cage again.

To the best of my knowledge, she never returned up to the top of the pool cage. But one night, unaware that she was resting on the windowsill outside of my bedroom, I accidently closed her in between the window and the screen!

She didn't get hurt, but after that, I don't think the window screen ever returned to its original shape.

I recall many times when I was practicing my violin, Sneaker would curl up inside my instrument case and fall asleep on its soft, furry lining.

She didn't care what I played, which notes I missed, or how many squeaks and scratches I made. She just wanted to be near me, and that was okay with me.

Sneaker was a gentle creature who loved everyone she met. Whether it was a human or another animal, she loved them all and they loved her.

I remember the time when we adopted a small black-and-white kitten we named Cuddles. Cuddles was born in a cabinet on our porch. Her mother was a shelter cat whom we had fostered from the local humane society until she gave birth to her kittens.

Once momma cat and her kittens were returned to the shelter to find their forever homes, Sneaker stepped right in and played the role of a surrogate mother. She protected the newly adopted kitten and, many times, could be found resting with Cuddles sleeping soundly on her back with her little paws softly hugging Sneaker's neck. It was an absolutely precious sight!

In my home, the Christmas holiday is always a special time, especially when shared with our furry pets. Without exception, every year, the cats love to watch me decorate the Christmas tree, as well as to sniff and check out all of the boxes containing the ornaments and decorations.

Unfortunately, over the years, the tree fell victim to the artistic work of a couple of naughty kitties. There were many opportunities, while we were either sleeping or out of the house, for the tree to be used as a giant jungle gym by one or more of the kitties. Many times, we would find broken and shattered ornaments on the floor, and some of the light strings pulled far away from the limbs of the tree. I'm not going to name any suspects, but I had my suspicions as to who the culprits were.

I don't think Sneaker ever participated in any of these shenanigans because she could always be found curled up and sleeping soundly next to the trunk of the Christmas tree on the soft, red, furry tree skirt that surrounded its base. Just like the furry lining inside my violin case, she enjoyed the solitude and tranquility that could be found every year under the Christmas tree.

By Christmas morning, all of the naughty behavior would be quickly forgotten, and the cats were delighted to receive a stocking of their own that included their favorite canned food, crunchy treats, and a few new catnip toys.

The remainder of the day would be spent watching the cats play with all the discarded gift wrap and bows strewn about the floor by the happy recipients of those gifts.

As the years passed by and Sneaker grew older, I began to wonder how long she would be with me here on earth. I can remember a day at the veterinarian's office when a lady who was there with her animal asked about Sneaker and specifically inquired about how old she was.

"Oh, 14 years old, you won't have many years left with her," the lady said to me when I told her Sneaker's age. I didn't reply, but thought to myself, "What a callous thing to say."

My thought at the time was that Sneaker would be with me for a very long time. After all, she had always been healthy.

But soon, Sneaker seemed to be slowing down. I would often find her resting quietly under a small shade tree just outside of the front door, and most evenings she could be found resting her aged and arthritic body on the hot stones that had been heated by the daytime sun.

Occasionally, Sneaker could be spotted sprinting across the back yard as if she were years younger. And as I watched her in amazement, a little voice inside reminded me that she was getting older and that these infrequent sprints across the yard were merely attempts to recapture her youth and energy of years past.

When Sneaker was around twenty years old, she became very ill and we took her to the veterinarian.

After an examination and some blood tests, it was determined that she was suffering from a thyroid disorder.

The veterinarian told me that her thyroid disease was very serious and that it was very important to keep her on medication. He discussed special radiation treatment that was available in another town that could help her, but it would be risky for her because of her age. During the treatment, he explained, she would have to remain in isolation for up to three weeks.

After weighing the options, I decided that the treatment and the time in isolation would be too difficult for Sneaker and me, and I chose to give her daily medication to control her symptoms.

I took her home and loved and cared for her.

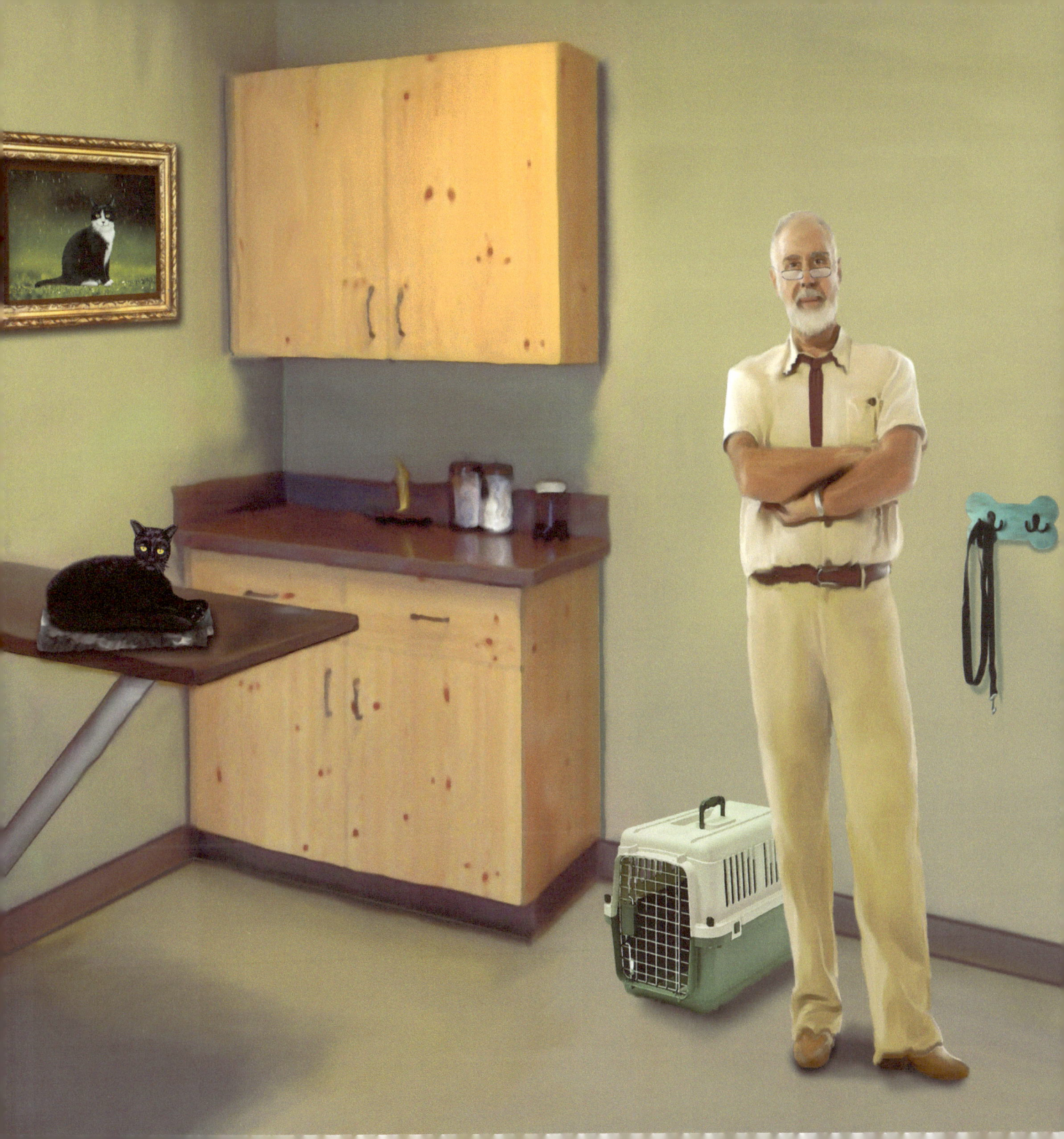

Sneaker lived for another two years after she was diagnosed. When the end of her life was near, I kept her comfortable, served her favorite foods, and LOVED her.
 We were together until the very end...the promise that I had made to her on the day I had adopted her.

Sneaker was a little more than twenty years old when she died. It is unusual for a cat to live that length of time. As a testimony, I believe that the care and the love that I gave her all of those years, contributed to her living such a long, healthy life. And I think that Sneaker loved me so darn much that she tried everything in her power to stay with me here on earth. The bond that we shared was unlike any I had ever experienced with an animal.

The days following her passing were filled with so much grief. It was paralyzing. I was absolutely devastated by her death. Even though I had had a couple of years to prepare for that day, it seemed like I wasn't prepared at all when it finally happened. That can happen when you lose someone you love so dearly.

My family understood my grief. Some of my friends, on the other hand, were cruel to the point of suggesting that I should never own another pet because I become too emotionally attached. That was when I realized that one should be careful with whom one shares stories of pet loss grief. Not everyone is an animal lover and I can respect that. It doesn't mean that they are no longer my friends; it just means that unless they have owned and loved a pet, they can't understand the sadness surrounding such a heartbreaking event.

At times when I find myself missing Sneaker and am particularly sad, I receive great comfort from reading a poem called The Rainbow Bridge. Just opposite this page is a copy of the poem. Once you read it, you will understand why it gives me such comfort and why I share it with others who are dealing with the loss of a beloved pet and why I wholeheartedly believe that Sneaker, a small, black, adopted cat with a big heart, my shadow for so many years, is waiting for me at a place called The Rainbow Bridge.

Until we meet again, Sneaker, I love you and will never forget you.

The Rainbow Bridge

Just this side of heaven is a place called Rainbow Bridge.

When an animal dies that has been especially close to someone here, that pet goes to Rainbow Bridge. There are meadows and hills for all of our special friends so they can run and play together. There is plenty of food, water and sunshine, and our friends are warm and comfortable.

All the animals who had been ill and old are restored to health and vigor. Those who were hurt or maimed are made whole and strong again, just as we remember them in our dreams of days and times gone by. The animals are happy and content, except for one small thing; they each miss someone very special to them, who had to be left behind.

They all run and play together, but the day comes when one suddenly stops and looks into the distance. His bright eyes are intent. His eager body quivers. Suddenly he begins to run from the group, flying over the green grass, his legs carrying him faster and faster.

You have been spotted, and when you and your special friend finally meet, you cling together in joyous reunion, never to be parted again. The happy kisses rain upon your face; your hands again caress the beloved head, and you look once more into the trusting eyes of your pet, so long gone from your life but never absent from your heart.

Then you cross Rainbow Bridge together...

–Author Unknown

www.ingramcontent.com/pod-product-compliance
Lightning Source LLC
Chambersburg PA
CBHW041533040426
42446CB00002B/74